Love Notes

Love Notes

Dear Husband,
I Appreciate You

Feels Like Fun ® Publications

David & Amanda Reigle

Feels Like Fun ® Publications

Fun Stuff.

Love Notes: Dear Husband, I Appreciate You.

This book and these Love Notes are part of a marriage series consisting of books, journals, podcasts and other art. This series was created by the founders of Feels Like Fun® LLC; David and Amanda Reigle. This book of love notes is intended to be written and drawn in. Images of the Feels Like Fun® Shoulder Panda™ mascot may be seen throughout the marriage series.

This journal is also part of the materials offered within the www.feelslikefun.com/wonderful membership consisting of online course content and social community. The Feels Like Fun® LLC "Wonderful" podcast series was released in 2024. Join now at feelslikefun.com/wonderful.

Join now to claim a discount on your membership. Create a fun, thoughtful and intimate experience for your marriage journey, together. Email us a copy of your proof of purchase to claim your discount today.
branding@feelslikefun.com #LoveNotes

This book of love notes is a marriage investment. It is a wonderful wedding gift and/or anniversary gift and it is intended to be used both for manifestation and connection. This book is great for individuals who are still manifesting a connection with their own favorite partner as well as committed daters and married couples. **Pardon our use of our pronouns. Include yourself.** There is no exclusion. Write your own love notes to represent your experience. **We love you.**

About the Authors

David Reigle is a co-founder of Feels Like Fun® LLC and the Feels Like Fun® Publications company. He is also a co-author of EBB & Flow™ couples devotional and the I Appreciate You™ journal series. He is a dedicated husband and loving father who leads with honor and empathy. He is a good man who respects himself and others. Those who know him say that he thinks before he speaks. He prays in authority, covering his loved ones under grace and in the most perfect way. He consistently gives of himself and appreciates every opportunity to bring grace and peace to his family and work. His diligent, generous, and gentle heart is determined to show compassion towards those whom he takes care of. He is intelligent and thoughtful to encourage his family toward their goals. He is a reliable source of patient wisdom. #Reiglelife #senpai #◈◇ #FeelsLikeFun® #FeelsLikeFun

Amanda Reigle is a co-founder of Feels Like Fun® LLC and the Feels Like Fun® Publications company. She is also a co-author of EBB & Flow™ couples devotional and the I Appreciate You™ journal series. She is a devoted wife and a gracious mother. She is a business-person, an author and an artist. Amanda enjoys collaborating with her husband, David, to create and sell digital products and other merchandise. Amanda's art and passions are an expression of her love for the cybernetics of human communications. She enjoys being part of building Feels Like Fun communications space both online and in person. She enjoys her family and pursuing her interests. #Reiglelife #kōhai #◈ ◇ #FeelsLikeFun® #FeelsLikeFun

Dear Beautiful kind strong diligent husband,

The joy that I experience, in peace with you, each new morning and night is my favorite gift in life so far. Thank you for blessing me every morning and night.

I ♡ U

Love, Me

I appreciate you. Thank you for being such a beautiful example of diligence and consistency. I adore you, love and grace is with us, always.

Love, Me

Dear Husband,

Thank you for taking care of our needs, physically, emotionally, spiritually. I love all the things that you are the best parent and partner, more satisfying than I ever imagined.

I love you.

Love, Me

Breath and Life Eternal,

Thank you for guiding us and being with us and in everything that we do. Thank you for a husband that I am drawn to; someone who I trust and believe in. You continue to be with my husband as he goes about his life and into forever.

Shalom.

Love, Me

Dear Husband,

I am appreciating your personality and authority more and more each day. Thank you for always finding time to still come and get a kiss and for always being honest. I want you and I am thankful that you share yourself with me.

Love, Me

Breath and Life Eternal,

Thank you for my husband's love. Thank you for continuing to be with him every moment as he guides our family. I love his authority, in alignment with perfect grace. Shalom.

♡ **Love, Me** ♡

Breath and Life Eternal,

Thank you for my wonderful, kind, handsome, smart husband. He takes such good care of us and does it with love. Thank you for protecting him wherever he goes, thank you for making him so very well.

Love, Me

Breath and Life Eternal,

Thank you for the constant and continued health and healing for everyone. Thank you to my husband for living a healthy and honest life. I am saturated in appreciation for the wisdom that resides within my husband as he guides us.

Shalom.

Love, Me

Dear Universe,

I am thankful to my husband for always looking to the Lord when we are in the times of need. I am thankful that I have been given this life to share with the type of man that our family can trust and rest beneath.

My husband is a good man. I love him.

Love, Me

My Love,

You are so brilliant. I am amazed at how easily you can do things that I do not even understand. Thank you for teaching me about patience and consideration by your example. You are my hero.

Love, Me

To my trusted partner,

Thank you for covering our family in your love and discipline. I appreciate your time and attention on any issues that we get to go through together. We submit this home in our hearts to your loving discipline. Shalom.

Love, Me

Dear Universe,

I appreciate this perfect and abundant world. I appreciate how this world works. Everything is working for our good. I appreciate the opportunity to love my husband. I appreciate my husband and his wisdom. May he be encouraged, today and always, Shalom.

Love, Me

My Love,
Thank you for always taking your time to make decisions for our family. I appreciate how you are quick to make slow decisions about serious things. I love you so much.
Love, Me

My Love,
Thank you for being a wonderful person. I can go to you with any feeling, and it will all workout for good. You are my hero. You saved the day for me yesterday with your love and understanding. I love you.
Love, Me

Dear Husband,
You are always saving the day, each and every day. You are my hero. Thank you for fixing my_____ You are so smart. I love being your wife. May you continue to be blessed, all day, every day.
Love, Me

Dear Husband,

You are the most beautiful, brilliant provider to us. Not only do you feed our bodies, but you feed our hopes and dreams. Thank you for always believing in me and my dreams and thank you for dreaming with me.

I adore you.

Love, Me

I appreciate my husband,

This man seeks access to more grace and wisdom each day. My husband finds and shares every good thing with me. His attention is so satisfying to my spirit, flesh and soul. I love him.

♡ **Love, Me** ♡

Dear Universe,

May I continue to learn how to be the best partner, wife and friend for my husband's highest satisfaction, Shalom.

Love, Me

My love,

Thank you for appreciating this journey of life with me. It is more beautiful every day with you. You are my best friend and I love to do all the things with you. Thank you for taking care of us and making us feel special and loved. You are a very kind and wise dad, and we love you. I hope you get to realize all your hopes and dreams soon.

♡ **Love, Me**

I appreciate my husband's kind and gentle personality.

I appreciate his alignment so that he is confident to cover and teach us. I appreciate that we both desire to rest in wisdom and grace and we do not expect the other partner to solve our own personal contrast in life. I love alignment and I love my husband.

Love, Me

Every morning and every night,

My husband verbally speaks love and progression over our family and offers appreciation for my presence in his life as his wife. I cannot express how much this consistency means to me. I appreciate how my husband is so very fun to me. I adore him.

He Loves Me

Dear Husband,

Thank you for finding offense in nothing and speaking life over me. Thank you for valuing both of our opinions before making decisions for our family. Thank you for your diligence and consistency. I appreciate your love.

Love, Me

Dear Husband,
YAY!

My name has changed! I am now officially

_____ !

Thank you for being the kind of person whose name I want to share. We are so blessed to love and cherish each other. Thank you for allowing me to know you this way. I love you.

Love, Me

Dear Husband,

Thank you for your diligence and consistency. You take such wonderful care of our family. I appreciate you very much. Have a wonderful day. I love you.

Love, Me

To the daddy of this house,

Thank you for always choosing to love when you are considering discipline for me and our children. We look to you for our identity in our own Breath and Life Eternal, and I am comforted by your loving authority. I appreciate you.

Love, Me

Dear Universe,

I appreciate a husband who aligns himself with grace and mercy first. This person is capable and willing to receive wisdom to guide our family in pursuit of our most satisfying experiences. It is so nice to appreciate how he is so good to us in the calm confidence of Shalom. He makes us feel safe.

Love, Me

Dear Husband,

No matter where you go or what you choose to do, I will love you there, where you are. You are the best person that I have ever known. I am honored to be yours. Thank you for loving our family so well.

Love, Me

My Love,

I hope that you have a peaceful day today, and every day. May there be a pink bubble of protection around you as you go to work. I appreciate your diligence. Thank you for being so consistent. I like thinking about positive vibes for everyone in your path. I love you.

♡ **Love, Me** ♡

Thank you to my sweet husband.

Thank you for how you always give us love that comes from your connection with the Breath and Life Eternal. Thank you for blessing our days and for always prioritizing your alignment with grace and Shalom every day. I love you, my husband.

Love, Me

Dear Husband,

I am grateful for all of the opportunities that I am given to rest in your arms. Thank you for always giving me kind directions. Thank you for being trustworthy and gentle. You are so funny. I like you a lot.

♡ **Love, Me**

Dear Universe,

I appreciate the perfection of all creation. I enjoy balance and hope. I appreciate how my husband stands strong and at peace.

Always, Shalom.

Love, Me

My Brilliant Husband,

You are our wonderful hero. I am grateful that you were going out and diligently serving our community. I'm proud of you. I love you.

Love, Me

We are Partners,

We rise in love. You are our hero. You are brilliant and kind. Yesterday, when there was a child sized pile of tears in your arms, I became more deeply in love with you than I can express with words. Thank you.

Love, Me

Dear Husband,

Thank you for your consistency and fun. You're always choosing to give us a strong and steady place to rest. We appreciate you so much. You are brilliant. And you're my hero, I love you deeply.

♡ **Love, Me**

My Love,

Thank you for being gracious. Even though you have to be firm, I appreciate your authority and all the other ways that you show us all the ways that you love us. Thank you for your diligent work to provide and care for us. Thank you for the freedom and encouragement to pursue my dreams. I love you.

♡ **Love, Me**

Lover,

I appreciate how you are so funny. You always make me laugh and know exactly what I need. Your touch is like a taste of Breath and Life Eternal and your smell gives me so much Shalom. Thank you for always being honest and for communicating with me about everything. You are an incredible dad and brilliant man. I adore you.

Love, Me

Husband,

You are the most wonderful man. I am fully satisfied in your arms as your wife. May your health and safety meet you in a fresh and new way all day, every day. I adore you.

Love, Me

Husband,

Thank you for helping me when I need it. I appreciate everything you do. I'm excited to think about this family that we have built together. I hope today is a wonderful day for you. I love you.

Love, Me

Husband,

I love being your wife. Thank you for always believing in my dreams. Thank you for being diligent in all you do. We ♡ U.

Love, Me

To my husband,

♡ Your breath is like candy to me. Your words are treasures to my heart as I focus upon the beautiful creation that is you. Thank you for sharing yourself with me. I adore you.

Love, Me

Dear Universe,

I appreciate this new day, married and well with my husband. He honors our family and always seeks to be graceful and wise. Here is a good example of a man after the heart of Breath and Life Eternal. We adore my husband's authority under grace and in the most perfect way. May he continue to be blessed in all that he does.

Shalom

♡ **Love, Me**

Dear Universe,

I desire to be closer and more intimate with my own connection to Breath and Life Eternal. I appreciate the opportunity and responsibility to take care of this special piece of eternity that exists within my husband. I appreciate the time that he invests in our relationship as we live together in real life. I see grace and mercy pouring out of him every day. I am with him all day, every day. I am so thankful that he is blessed as he goes into the world. Shalom.

♡ **Love, Me**

Husband,

I appreciate the way that you stop and think before you make decisions for our family. Your wisdom makes us feel safe. Thank you for staying humble in your royalty. Everything is always working out for you.

Love, Me

My Love,

You are my best friend and my favorite person. Thank you for leading us in this satisfying life. I love you.

♡ **Love, Me**

Dear husband,

I'm so thankful that I can wake up from a bad dream and it's you I wake up to... you are the most wonderful man I've ever known. Thank you. Love your wife.

♡ **Love, Me** ♡

My wonderful husband,

Thank you for always taking the time to pay close attention to us. Thank you for giving us new ways to feel your love, you are our brilliant hero. We adore you. Thank you.

Love, Me

My husband,

You are my home. My favorite place to be is in your arms. Thank you for always making us feel safe and calm. You are protected in all ways, and always, Shalom. I love you.

Love, Me

My love,

Thank you for always talking to me about the decisions that you are making. I love being on your team. You are very wise. I trust you. I also think that you are so funny.

♡ **Love, Me**

Dear Husband,

Thank you for making our family feel safe. You always look to the father for us to find our security and it brings us so much satisfaction and joy. You are a kind man. Thank you for disciplining us in a supportive and gentle way. I adore you.

Love, Me

Dear Husband,

You are the kindest, most wise man that I have ever known. Thank you for always making me laugh and for always inspiring me to new satisfaction. I adore you. May your days be full of fresh and interesting stuff. I love you.

Love, Me

Husband,

Your heart is my home. Thank you for being so fun and for parenting with me with confidence. I love you.

♡ **Love, Me**

My Love,
I adore you. Thank you for leading us in love.
Love, Me

Husband,
I adore you. You are my favorite person to be around. You are about doing and being a good person. I admire you and I appreciate how you care for us.
Love, Me

Dear Husband,
I really appreciate your Love and Attention. You are my best friend, and you are a wonderful friend to me. Thank you for encouraging me and enjoying me. I ♡ you.
Love, Me

Dear Husband,
I love you so very much. Thank you.
Love, Me

To the King of our Home,
Thank you for operating under grace, in the most perfect way. Thank you for being a strong, kind, brave man with a strong personal conviction through all of the trials or contrast. Thank you for being a gentleman, always. Your heart + soul are my home. Thank you for taking such wonderful care of us.
♡ **Love, Me** ♡

Husband,
Thank you for teaching me about obedience in love. Being your wife is the desire of my heart, realized. Your company, authority and joy are **treasures** that I cherish.
Love, Me

Dear Husband,

You are so attractive. I love it when you say sweet things to me. I love how you share your beautiful

_____

with me. I love it when you make jokes. I love it when you're serious... I just really LOVE YOU.

Love, Me

Dear Husband,

Thank You for being so kind to us. Thank you for being diligent in bringing our attention to personal accountability. I trust you and appreciate all your authority in our home.

Love, Me

Husband,

I am so thankful for the time we have together. You are my best friend. Thank you for loving us.

Love,

Love, Me

Husband,
You are my best friend. I adore you and your hilarious personality. Thank you for always finding the fun. YOU ROCK!
Love, Me

YOU ARE MY FAVORITE.
I AM SO APPRECIATIVE OF ALL THAT YOU ARE. THANK YOU FOR LOVING OUR FAMILY. THANK YOU FOR GIVING US SOMEWHERE BEAUTIFUL AND FUN TO BELONG. YOU ARE A KIND AND WISE + I LOVE YOU. YOU ARE AMAZING.
Love, Me

My Husband,
You are marvelous. You are beautiful and strong. Your kindness makes me strong, and I love sharing life with you. Thank you for loving and protecting us. ♡ we adore you.
Love, Me

Dear Husband,

Thank you for our home and happy life together. Thank you for loving us so very well. You are so full of love. It amazes me how much I enjoy your company. Thank you for being your authentic self with me. Please always tell me what you're feeling. I adore you.

♡ **Love, Me** ♡

Dear Husband,

Thank you for being kind and gentle when we need that kind of love. Thank you for being solid and steadfast when we need that kind of love. Thank you for being fun and joyful with me. I adore you.

Love, Me

Dear Husband,

You are my favorite person to be around!

♡ **Love, Me** ♡

Dear Husband,

You are the Head of this Household.

You chose to be the leader in our home, and I am thankful every day. Thank you for loving us and for seeing us as worthy to be loved. You amaze me with your wisdom and mercy every day.

♡ **Love, Me**

Hubby,

I ♡ your_____, and your face and your muscles and your _____. and your toes. I ♡ U so much. I ♡ your knees and your skills + your dreams. I ♡ your faith and I ♡ your love. Thank you for giving us a place to belong with you.

♡ **Love, Me**

Dear Lover,

I adore you. You are such a wonderful role model, leader, and father. Waking up to you and falling asleep with you is such a great wealth that I appreciate it more each day. I ♡ U.

Love, Me

Dear Husband,
Thank you for **ALWAYS** being so kind and for being fun. I enjoy being your wife. **Love, Me**

Dear Husband,
I ♡ being your wife. I ♡ waking up with you, going to sleep with you & doing life with you.
   ♡ **your wife**

TO THE LOVE OF MY LIFE,
YOUR BREATH IS THE HAPPIEST THING TO ME. I CELEBRATE A LIFETIME OF LOVE WITH YOU. THANK YOU FOR LOVING ME SO WELL. I TRUST THE FATHER TO BRING US EVERY GOOD THING. WE NOW RECEIVE EVERY GOOD THING FROM THE FATHER UNDER GRACE AND IN THE MOST PERFECT WAY.
   ♡ **Love, Me** ♡

Dear Husband,

Being your wife... and your helper is my life's greatest honor. ☺ Thank you for allowing me to love you in all of the ways. I pray that I can learn more about how to be a better wife to you. ♡ Thank you for taking care of our family's hearts & teaching us about God. Shalom. I ♡ U

Love, Me

Dear Husband,

Thank you for being so kind and gentle during any problems. You are an amazing dad. I ♡ U

♡ **Love, Me**

My Love,

Your heart's desire is a gift from the Lord. Our Father in heaven is in you and desires for you to have and enjoy every good thing. May you now & forevermore receive his love with gladness ♡ I adore you.

♡ **Love, Me**

My Husband,
Thank you for always considering my opinions. Thank you for teaching me about GRACE & WISDOM. Your guidance and discipline are gifts unto our family from our heavenly Father.
♡ **Love, Me**

Dear Husband,
Thank you for loving us so well. You are the best dad & man I have ever known.
I ♡ U.
HAVE FUN.
♡ **Love, Me**

Daddy,
We are in a hurry today + I love you.
♡ **Love, Me**

Dear daddy of this family,

I make mistakes sometimes. I wonder what kind of angel you are because you seem so perfect to me. I want to be more like you. I deeply love you.

♡ **Love, Me**

Husband,

♡ I love being your wife... and your favorite secret agent. Thank you for your love.

♡ **Love, Me**

Dear_____**,**

I ♡ U.

Thank you for being such a kind, LOVING man. I am appreciating you more every day.

♡ **Love, Me**

Husband,
You are my best friend. I ♡ U.
♡ **Love, Me**

Dear Husband,
Thank you for loving us so well. Thank you for being so diligent in your work and in supporting us. Being yours is the greatest joy that I have had the opportunity to share with our Father God, Lord of All. I like to think about all of the adventures that we have had and will have, and the benefits that we are to the kingdom of the Lord in us and in this world.
♡ Forever ♡
Love, Me

Dear Husband,
I love to groom and ride you. You are a super _____. I love being yours. Thank you for being fun and nice and always being helpful.
I ♡ U
♡ **Love, Me**

Daddo,

Thank you for having the Father's Heart for our family. Your love & grace heals us every day. I pray the Lord shows us how we can bless you, more and more, as we all grow as a family. I ♡ U

♡ **Love, Me**

I AM THAT I AM

Thank you for guiding us. Thank you for always going before us as individuals and as a family and carving out the way for us to allow our most perfect experience under your grace and in the most perfect way. We love you.

♡ **Love, Me**

♡ **To my wonderful beautiful kind man,**

I adore you. You are the king of our home. Thank you for choosing me to partner with as we choose our father together in this life.

Thank you.

I ♡ U

♡ **Love, Me**

Father God,

Thank you for making my husband and I enjoy life together. Thank you for the satisfaction in walking up together healthy, wealthy and wise. Thank you for the Joy and appreciation for each other.

♡ **Love, Me**

Dear Husband,

I love you. Thank you for being so kind and for being so gentle when your wisdom calls for you to teach us... I love learning from you. Thank you for your diligence.

♡ **Love, Me**

Dear Daddy of our home,

I love you. I hope you have a wonderful day. You are my hero, and I am very thankful for your counsel. I'm looking forward to learning more in life with you.

♡ **Love, Me**

My love,

Thank you for this beautiful life together. You are my hero and I love being your wife. You are brilliant.

♡ **Love, Me**

Father Lord God of All,

I praise you and your Grace And wisdom, for the perfection of my beautiful husband. It's my pleasure to be his wife and we choose to love and honor you; the I AM THAT, I AM, first and for eternity. We choose you as one. We love you so much.

♡ **Love, Me**

YOU ARE MY HERO,

Thank you for my kind, gentle , generous and hilarious husband who prioritizes YOU; Lord, Father God of all, as our source of peace, communication, and hope and joy. He is my hero under grace and in the most perfect way.

Shalom

♡ **Love, Me**

My Love,

Thank you for this beautiful life with you and our Father, God; Lord of all. You are the most wonderful man I have ever met. Being your wife is my favorite thing about this life, under grace, in the most perfect way. I ♡ to think about our health, wealth + happiness. I ♡ U.

 ♡ **Love, Me**

Dear Husband,

Going all the places is always an adventure with you. Being anywhere with you at any time is fun. I love being your wife. I love learning from you and sharing myself with you. No person has ever made me feel safer and more at home. I love you. Father Lord of all; Bless my husband always and in all the ways.

 ♡ **Love, Me**

Dear Husband,

Thank you for your love. I am so thankful that you chose to love this family and lead us, under grace and in the most perfect way. I love to learn from you. I love to be best friends with you and I love your body with my body. You are a brilliant, majestic man. My hero. I ♡ U

 ♡ **Love, Me**

My love,

Today I was thinking about our son someday saying that it is hard to find a woman who respects him the way that I respect you and I saw myself saying that I am a wild woman who respects you the way I do because of WHO YOU ARE and how YOU LIVE. You are an amazing example. I ♡ U

♡ **Love, Me**

My love,

I am in awe of your goodness, faithfulness, gentleness and kindness. I'm in awe of your love, your self-control, peace, and your patience. ♡ Thank you for being kind to us. Thank you for making this house a home and for making us feel at home wherever you are. You are the wisest man I have ever known... that I have ever even known of. You amaze me every day. You are brilliant and you are our hero. I adore you.

♡ **Love, Me**

Dear Husband,

I love you and I am in love with your beautiful soul. I am so thankful for your attention... and your butt. XOXO

♡ **Love, Me**

My love,

You are amazing and brilliant. Thank you for protecting us by taking good care of yourself, your body, your soul and your relationship with our father. We trust and ADORE you.

♡ **Love, Me**

Dear Husband,

You are the kindest, most gentle man I've ever known. I am SAFE, our family is SAFE with you. Thank you for loving us so well. I know you love me and our family, and that is the wealthiest feeling that I have ever had.

♡ **Love, Me**

Father God,

Thank you for blessing my husband with wisdom. Thank you that we trust him and love to be led by him. Shalom.

♡ **Love, Me**

Lovely Husband,

You are so kind and wise. Thank you for caring about my feelings. You are a very good man. We love you.

♡ **Love, Me**

Heavenly Father,

Thank you for a husband who loves you. Thank you for being inside my husband and for always loving him and keeping him safe, happy, balanced and healthy. Thank you, Father God, for sharing your joy through my husband.

♡ **Love, Me**

My Love,

Thank you for being so consistent. You are the most satisfying person to be around. Everybody loves you because you are incredible. I adore you.

♡ **Love, Me**

Dear Husband,

Thank you for loving us. Thank you for being patient and kind with us. I think you are very funny + fun + I love your opinions.

♡ **Love, Me**

Dear Husband,

I love you. You are the best husband in the whole world. Thank you for being you and for sharing yourself with us... I adore you.

♡ **Love, Me**

My love,

Thank you for being a kind loving man who takes care of our Spirits + Souls. Thank you for taking care of my heart. I adore you and all the things about you.

I love you.

♡ **Love, Me**

Dear Husband,

I love that you dared to take our family as your own. My husband is my hero! Thank the Lord Father God of All for putting us together to love and cherish each other. My husband is wise and kind and I adore him. He is brilliant. ♡

♡ **Love, Me**

Dear loving husband,

Your_____ is so gorgeous.

Your _____ is so pretty.

Your face is so handsome.

Your spirit is so peaceful.

Your body is so lovely.

Your eyes are so beautiful.

Your words are so perfect.

Your laugh is my favorite.

I love you.

♡ **Love, Me**

Dear Beautiful loving kind sweet strong husband,

I adore you. Thank you for being such a kind father + man to us. We look up to you.

♡ **Love, Me**

Dear wonderful husband,

Thank you for understanding that no one is perfectly behaved all the time. Thank you for caring about the words I have to say and the way I feel. I adore you and I pray for your continued happiness to be realized by you.

I ♡ you.

♡ **Love, Me**

My love,

Thank you for being my friend. I love talking to you and hugging you. You are amazing.

♡ **Love, Me**

Dear Husband,

I appreciate how you have become so brilliant. You are my hero. Thank you for loving us so well and for being graceful and perfect in every way. You are a strong, wise and kind man made up of all things that are good.

♡ **Love, Me**

Dear Husband,

I adore you and I really appreciate your attention and love. Thank you for being good to us. We learn more from you every day About how to be awesome and happy and full of grace. I ♡ U.

♡ **Love, Me**

My love,

Thank you for loving us so well. I'm so impressed with what you do! You are amazing! Come home to me and kiss me. I love you **so much.**

♡ **Love, Me**

Daddo,

Thank you for being a beautiful example to our family + the world of what a good man, husband + father is. I adore you + I respect you + I appreciate you.

♡ **Love, Me**

Dearest Husband,
You're the best man I've ever known. You are my treasure... my safe, loving, funny, fun, kind husband. I'm thankful for every moment we have together. I adore you.
♡ **Love, Me**

Dear Husband,
I love being your wife. I appreciate all the things you do and say to help us know that we belong. ♡
♡ **Love, Me**

Daddo,
You are so handsome. You are so beautiful. You are so holy, under grace and in the most perfect way. ♡
♡ **Love, Me**

To the source of all eternal creation,
Thank you for gracing me with yourself manifested into my life as my husband and all the beautiful blessings that I get to see, smell, hear, taste, touch as I go through life with him. You are so good to us. I love you.
♡ **Love, Me**

My love,
Thank you for being a wonderful and kind representation of all the Father; "I AM" deserves to give and do for us as a family (and as individuals in his love). I desire to be a fruitful and satisfying representation of the Father's love for you. Thank you for loving us. You are my hero. You are a brilliant man and I simply adore you.
♡ **Love me**

Lover,
. I like knowing that we belong together. I adore you.
♡ **Love, Me**

Dear Husband,

You are the most amazing man + dad + husband + lover. I love you. Thank you for looking into your vacation days! How Fun! I can't wait to get to spend extra time together.

♡ **Love, Me**

Dear Husband,

I hope some of your wisdom rubs off on me. ♡♡♡ You are so wise and kind. Thank you for being who you are. I pray that each day that I unfold into a woman who brings you more pleasure each day. I enjoy your happiness the most. Shalom

♡ **Love, Me**

Dear Husband,

Someone needs to write you a **BIG** check because you deserve it! You are the best husband in the world.

I ♡ your breath. ♡ ♡ ♡ You are my best friend. I ♡ U

♡ **Love, Me**

To the source of all eternal creation,

Thank you for blessing us. Thank you for bringing my husband and I together. Thank you for our family, and the unconditional love that we have for each other; under grace and in the most perfect way. I pray that you; To the source of all eternal creation, will be glorified through us. May my husband co- create another amazing day with you today at work. Shalom

♡ **Love, Me**

Dear Husband,

Thank you for comforting us. Thank you for bedtime stories and basketball and cars and cards and video games. Thank you for meds on time and doing dishes after dinner. Thank you for being calm when things are hard. Thank you for doing life together. P.S. May the source of all eternal creation and our time in it, allow me to continue to become a better wife to you each day. I adore you.

♡ **Love, Me**

Dearest husband,

Your company and presence are my favorite things to appreciate. Thank you for loving us so well. To the source of all eternal creation is with you always.

I ♡ U.

♡ **Love, Me**

Dear Husband,

Your beautiful_____ and your

_____ are totally epic.

I love you.

♡ **Love, Me**

To the source of all eternal creation,

Thank you for who and what I am. I praise you for making me. I praise you for making my husband. I praise you for blessing and guiding our family. I praise you for my husband's perfectly made (and well cared for) body and mind. I praise you for his authority and discipline over us to remain steadily within you. Shalom

♡ **Love, Me**

Daddo,

We are all in a rush to get out of the house today, but I just like to make time to say thank you....

So ... THANK YOU.

♡ **Love, Me**

Daddo,
Nobody else can calm and comfort me or
_____ like you can. Nobody knows me like
you do. I like it.
 ♡ **Love, Me**

Father Lord God of All,
Thank you for my beautiful husband and his gentle, strong, kind, sturdy, steady and reliable love. Thank you for inspiring him to touch me the way that he does. So amazing to share myself and my body with you through my husband. He is amazing under grace, and in the most perfect way. I belong to him, in you. Shalom.
 ♡ **Love, Me**

Dear Husband,
I appreciate your courage when it comes to leading our family in unending love and forgiveness. I love that you are our leader. I do not want to ever try to lead this family without your blessing. You are a way better leader, and you bless us with your leadership. ♡
 ♡ **Love, Me**

Dear Husband,

Thank you for caring about my emotions... And for offering me grace to pardon my faults. I think you are the most wonderful, kind, loving, and respectful husband and I am sorry that I acted selfish and bratty yesterday. **I was wrong** and I am so thankful for your forgiveness. I love you.

♡ **Love, Me**

Hello my love,

Thank you for sharing yourself with me. I love and appreciate everything you do to care for me and this family. I love thinking about you having a great day.

I ♡ U

♡ **Love, Me**

To my wonderful and kind husband,

Your love is a beautiful flower, with life everlasting. Each day you are like a new Bloom of love in me, under our Father God Almighty. I am so thankful that I have freedom to praise the Lord.

I ♡ U

♡ **Love, Me**

Dear Husband,

Loving you is such a wonderful gift. You are beautiful, kind and sweet. You are good, gentle and funny. You are a man who knows who he is and is confident. Your peace and grace give us a home. May I be blessed with a long life loving you no longer has children of Our Lord father God. Apartment with you in all things. I trust you. I am yours.

I ♡ U

♡ **Love, Me**

To my dear, loving, kind, understanding husband,

Thank you for gently understanding when I have made a mistake. You are so kind, and it gives me the freedom to desire to honor you to my best ability. I pray that the Lord continues to teach me within your love and covering. I love being your wife. I hope you have a beautiful day. Thank you, my love.

♡ **Love, Me**

Dear Husband,

I like thinking about things that you enjoy. I like thinking about building a bog garage together and watching you fix and explore all the fun things.

Love, Me

Father God,

Thank you for my husband. Thank you for his love and for our safety. You are a good father to us, and we see your love for us through him every day. Thank you for always going before us and preparing a fun and peaceful way for us to go.

Shalom

♡ **Love, Me**

Dear Husband,

I love you and your_____ and your eyes,

and your _____ and your hands,

And your legs and arms and feet, your mind and soul and your knees. I love your beautiful knees. I ♡ U

♡ **Love, Me**

You are everything lovely, my dear sweet husband.

Thank you for believing in me in my dreams. Thank you for supporting our family with your good and generous efforts. You're so diligent and taking care of us spiritually, mentally, emotionally.... and to me... physically ♡. You are such a wonderful dad and husband, and also you are a very good son to your mother, and to your dad... And to the eternal source of all creation that is living within your own being.

I adore you.

♡ **Love, Me**

I reach out to the Almighty source of my being,
the "I AM" that is the source of all creation for all eternity:
I sing praise for my husband's epic personality.
I appreciate the thought of his happy days and his hopeful wise mind.
This man is my husband, and he is wonderful.
As I gaze upon him, I can see how the world is a good and kind and safe place.
I lift my voice in joy for this love that I have for my husband and his love for me.
Thank you to this world, for we receive your love for us.
We are good people and good things happen for us every day.
♡ **Love, Me**

The "I AM", You are the "Ego eimi" ; (Ancient Greek: ἐγώ εἰμι Greek pronunciation: [egɔ̌ː eːmí]) "I am", "I exist". I love to think of you in my husband and in my Self, together; as one, with all the other parts of "Ego eimi". Thank you for the opportunity to be in agreement with my husband about "Ego eimi".
Shalom
♡ **Love, Me**

Thank you for the Shalom.

Thank you for showing us that there is PEACE to be had and celebrated. Thank you for this knowing that Shalom is a celebration and surrender to your peace. Thank you that my husband brings Shalom to us all.

Shalom

♡ **Love, Me**

To my wonderful husband,

You are my wonderful, sweet, kind, beautiful man. Your attention and care are my sweet centering place, my home. Thank you for being patient and consistent with me. You are patient, responsible and wise.

♡ **Love, Me**

Dear Husband,

Thank you for how you see us; perfect and blameless. Thank you for giving us permission to feel good about ourselves. Thank you for this love and trust. Thank you for comfort and happiness. Thank you for offering more and more blessings for us to enjoy together each day.

♡ **Love, Me**

A thank you to my husband.

Thank you for caring for our home and our transportation and thank you for our love. You are my best friend on Earth and my favorite person ever. May all good and satisfying blessings come to you more and more forever.

♡ **Love, Me**

I AM

Thank you for my husband and his diligence to care for us. We are one. I see your love for us through his words and actions every day. My husband is so perfectly made and holds himself in your hands and I love to rest in that, with him. I love partnering with him. We agree to trust the I AM; The I AM who is the beginning and the end, Father of the whole universe, forever; for we are covered and cared for in all ways. Shalom

♡ **Love, Me**

Dear Husband,

You are very diligent and considerate, and I respect your time.

I ♡ U forever.

♡ your wife♡

Love, Me

Dear Husband,

Thank you for sharing your personality with us. Thank you for who you are and who you choose to be. You are the most wonderful companion and leader. Your gentle and wise kindness shows up in the way that you love and care for us every day. Your body is a temple where I can worship the glory of what has been made. I AM HERE TO THANK YOU for this JOY.

Shalom,

♡ **Love, Me**

Dear Husband,

I adore loving you. You are my best friend and being yours is my life's greatest treasure. I pray for your absolute continued and increasing satisfaction and pleasant joy. I am so proud that you are worthy of our respect and honor under grace in the most perfect way.

♡ **Love, Me**

My love,

Thank you for being my best friend and for all of your love. You are so trustworthy, and I feel safe with you. Thank you for taking care of us. I hope that you never stop trusting the "I AM that; I AM" when you seek wisdom.

♡ **Love, Me**

Dear Husband,

Thank you for taking care of yourself. Yes, I mean you. It is important to our family that you feel that all your desires are being realized, in a steady and consistent way that brings you joy under grace in the most perfect way. Thank you for budgeting for our family. I would like to never get over your beauty and goodness; inside and out.

♡ **Love, Me**

My Love,

Your ideas and humor are my favorite things to enjoy. Thank you for loving us so well.

Love, Me

Dear Husband,

You are my King. The Lord Father God of All gave me to you. You were given our family to reign over and care for. I love being your wife. Being your wife teaches me new things about myself and my relationship with the I AM, more and more every day. I'd be honored to live the rest of my life with you, under grace in the most perfect way.

♡ **Love, Me**

Dear Husband,

Thank you for guiding me and comforting me when I'm confused or upset. You always seem to know what I need. You take such good care of us and I appreciate you so much.

I ♡ U

♡ **Love, Me**

My love,

Thank you for being my beloved friend. Talking with you and laughing with you and listening to you are great and wonderful joys. I praise the Lord, Father God of all in ALL THAT YOU ARE. Thank you for always taking the time to listen to me about my feelings and thoughts.

I ♡ U

♡ **Love, Me**

My love,

Thank you to my amazing husband for loving me unconditionally and for always saying sweet things to me. You are the most precious gift to everyone who meets you! May your day be filled with productive joy. I adore you.

♡ **Love, Me**

Dear Husband,

I want to tell everyone about your beautiful knees, face ankles, toes, elbows, hands, heart, mind, ears, fingers, blood, tendons, bones, muscles, ligaments, cartilage, skin, _____ , and authority forever.

♡ **Love, Me**

Dear Husband,

You inspire me every day to be a stronger, wiser, kinder person. I believe in you. I trust you. I rest knowing your authority comes from the Lord, Father God of all. It is so good to love you and appreciate you more everyday. Thank you for being our leader. It takes a lot of faith and courage and hope to take care of us and love us like you do.

I ♡ U

♡ **Love, Me**

To my husband,

I adore you and I love writing you notes. I ♡ knowing that I can send you love when you're at work. I love thinking about how well you love us through the Father. I pray there is more that I can do to show you my love each day. You are brilliant.

♡ **Love, Me**

Father God,

Thank you for my husband and the diligence with which he cares for our hearts and minds. Thank you for his love and attention through you. Thank you for healthy, wealthy, happy, and fun time together and thank you for our productive and peaceful times when we are physically apart. My husband is a good man and I want to honor him today and tomorrow; forever. Bless his today and his always, in you Father. Shalom

♡ **Love, Me**

Father Lord God,

Thank you for my husband and for myself, and for our family. Thank you for humility and grace towards the families that we came from. Thank you for everything we have learned from them. Thank you for teaching us about your love as we go through this "time space, reality" together. ☺ This is a good life, and I am so happy to know, love and treasure my husband. Thank you for being with my husband all the time, showering us with your love and authority. Shalom.

♡ **Love, Me**

Dear Husband,

You are such a wonderful example to us about how to be a good person with a whole heart who is connected to the source of all eternal creation. Thank you for teaching us about true love in this "real" world. I ♡ U

You are my brilliant hero.

♡ **Love, Me**

To the source of all eternal creation,

Thank you for sharing my husband with me. Thank you for his life and how he knows you and loves you and is wise to seek your wisdom in his work and authority for our family. Thank you for his body and mind. Thank you for his love for me, and his love for himself. Thank you for blessing him with every good thing. Thank you for keeping him safe and having fun. Shalom.

$\heartsuit$ **Love, Me**

Husband,

I love watching you play with the kids in our life. I appreciate you for being my husband. I appreciate all of your love and attention. You are my favorite person and I love to think of your happiness. Thank you for your love and attention. Thank you for your_____
deep in my soul. Thank you for your arms wrapped around me. Shalom.

$\heartsuit$ **Love, Me**

Dear Husband,

Being your wife is my favorite thing. I love you so much. Your happiness is the best thing. I need your love so very much. I $\heartsuit$ U

$\heartsuit$ **Love, Me**

Dear Husband,

I appreciate you and your beauty and strength and kindness and wisdom. You're my best friend and I appreciate you so much. Thank you for loving us. Thank you for being a fun and sexy and kind and strong leader. I love your voice. I like it when you relax.

♡ **Love, Me**

Dear Husband,

It's so inspiring; the way you respond calmly and thoughtfully to all the different kinds of situations. You are the most glorious expression of the Father; under grace, and in the most perfect way. I am in awe of you and your wise peace in the Lord each day. I love you and I love to be in your arms. Thank you for being my husband and for being the Dad in our home.

♡ **Love, Me**

Dear Husband,

It is impressive that you prioritize time with your mom. I pray that the Lord blessed me as a mother, like your mom is blessed by you each day and every day. You are a very good man and I know your parents are so proud of you. I know God is pleased. I am pleased and I love you very much.

♡ **Love, Me**

My love,

I wish everyone could think before they speak like you do. Thank you for teaching me more every day about the grace and honor in having a wise and peaceful heart. Your influence and authority bless us more and more each day and every day. May you continue to realize the ways you are blessed and loved more and more for eternity.

♡ **Love, Me**

My love,

It blows my mind that you have such wonderful self-control. I want to be more like you. I am very thankful for your example. I know myself and I know that I become a better human everyday while in your care and under your authority. Thank you for always giving me grace and offering me humble and gentle forgiveness. You are my best friend and I adore you.

♡ **Love, Me**

My love,

I wish that I had known you were going to be my husband when I was a little girl. I feel so much comfort when I consider that out of my tears and broken heartedness you were created; as the most perfect man to love me, in the most perfect way. I see you as a true angel on Earth. I love you so much.

♡ **Love, Me**

My love,

Thank you for being so kind and gentle to _____ and I. Your peace and patience and grace becomes us and gives us a place to belong. You are the treasure that we have found in the Lord, Father God of all. I praise the Lord for your love. Shalom.

♡ **Love, Me**

My love,

It is awesome how you are never afraid to be honest with me. I love that we are honest with each other. I love thinking about being able to be ourselves together. I adore you and love spending time with you. Thank you for being the most amazing husband.

♡ **Love, Me**

Dear Husband,

Thank you for loving us and for always praying for us. You are an amazing man and husband and dad.

♡ **Love, Me**

Dear Lover,

Let's get weird later. I love how you do all the weird things with me and I think it is really fun how as a married couple we are free of shame or guilt as we try all the weird things we want to try, together. Being free and weird with you is cool. You are cool. P.S. I have a crush on your

♡ **Love, Me**

My Beloved,

I like how you always cover us in prayer. I like how you pray with me and with our family. You are so brilliant. Thank you for being our hero and for showing us your unconditional love. Your love comes from deep within you. I feel the love of the Father God; Lord of all come out of you to cover us more and more, every day. You are wise and I am blessed to honor and obey you. Shalom.

♡ **Love, Me**

Dear Lover,

You are my husband.

I love that. I love saying that. I love that we love living life together and that we love loving the Lord and our family, together. I respect and love you.

♡ **Love, Me**

Dear Husband,

Thank you for being so funny. I am so glad that you like to laugh. You're basically the funniest person I know, so that's good. I ♡ U

♡ **Love, Me**

Dear Husband,

Thank you for your love and attention. I love being your wife. I trust you. I believe in your integrity. I ♡ U

♡ **Love, Me**

Dear sweet and kind husband,

You are my very best friend. Thank you for always helping me grow (and grow up) into a more level human. You are the most wonderful daddy and husband. Thank you for being so responsible and diligent. I love to follow your authority, under grace in the most perfect way. I love that I don't have to be without your hugs and kisses and high fives.

♡ **Love, Me**

Dear Husband,

I appreciate your love and attention. You are so beautiful and kind and sexy, and I adore you. Thank you for taking such good care of us. I ♡ U

♡ **Love, Me**

Dear Husband,

Thank you for sharing your fun, sexy, kind, loving, smart, sweet, strong, comforting, diligent wise self with us. Being your wife is a happy, hopeful, fun experience. I really like you.

♡ **Love, Me**

Lover,

You make me a better person. I love learning about grace and honor by watching you. You are the most amazing husband to me, and I love being your wife. I like how you never steal, lie or give up on us.

♡ **Love, Me**

My love,

Thank you for your love and attention. Thank you for loving us and being our authority. You are our, "here". I love you so much.

♡ **Love, Me**

Dear husband,

I am amazed that you are patient and kind with me; always.

♡ **Love, Me**

Father, Lord God,

Thank you for my husband and his love. Thank you for my husband's peaceful and kind soul. Thank you that he aligns to teach me how to behave better and more pleasing to you, and him. Thank you for his love. Thank you for blessing him, always.

♡ **Love, Me**

Dear Husband,

Your company and attention are my favorite gifts from the Lord God of all. I appreciate every single touch, every word, every display of discipline, every laugh, every diligent moment, every wise plan; every breath that I get to share with you. My brilliant hero.

♡ **Love, Me**

My love,

Thank you for always keeping us safe and for teaching us how to be wise and safe. You are such a wonderful man and I appreciate that you are our authority under grace, in the most perfect way. Your face and body and hands and feet are so beautiful, and your arms keep me home. I pray that the Father; Lord God of all, is always rejoicing in our love.

♡ **Love, Me**

Father, Lord God of all,

We love you, and we appreciate your ever-present participation in our lives. I thank you for showing up for my husband in an intimate and fun way today and tomorrow and forever... You are our best friend.

You and I are one; under grace and in the most perfect ♡

Love, Me

Hey babe,

I adore you. You are my favorite person to listen to, talk to, smell, honor, taste and see. I respect and love you. You are my brilliant hero and I trust that you are in line with the Father Lord God of all for eternity. I trust you. I welcome your guidance and your direction. If you were a superhero, your superpower would be "wisdom"; guided by the Father Lord God of all. Shalom.

♡ **Love, Me**

To my beautiful husband,

Thank you for loving me. Thank you for being kind and understanding for caring about my feelings and for always giving me kisses. I adore you.

♡ **Love, Me**

Dear Loving Husband,

I know that you married me and became _____'s dad out of love and faith. I believe with all that I am that the Father Lord God of all is guiding you and giving you the emotions and tools that you need to succeed in him and in the most is possible ease along our path and time together. I trust you forever and I appreciate you forever. Each day as your wife is my favorite. I love you so much. You are so brave and faithful that you decided to be our family authority under grace and in the most perfect way.

♡ **Love, Me**

My love,

I appreciate how you listen to me and how you are willing to make the ease of our communication more powerful each day. It is very soothing to me to be able to obey and trust you. I love knowing that if you are tired and can't communicate with me effectively, that you will tell me. I love "lemon" and I love "banana" and I love all the new code words in the future that will give us freedom to communicate with greater ease in times of pressure. I love being your wife and I love you. You are our brilliant hero.

♡ **Love, Me**

My Love,

Your patience and kindness are legendary. You are my very best friend and favorite person. You are the most glorious manifestation of the father's attention. You have given us a priceless gift that is more valuable in any earthly thing. The Almighty, Lord God of all lives through your authority and love for us.

Shalom

♡ **Love, Me**

Husband,

Thank you for always speaking over our family and love and acceptance. I know we aren't perfect, but we are loved by you. That makes us better every day. I appreciate your authority.

Love, Me

Dear Husband,

You are an amazing man and a very funny friend and husband. I love your humor. I love that you are secure in yourself and capable of making silly jokes with me and your friends. I am thankful that you have friends that understand you. ♡ I am thankful that I get to spend my life being your wife. I love that I am getting to know you and love you more every-day as we walk through all the things together. You're my husband and the most beautiful, brilliant, perfect hero. We love you.

♡ **Love, Me**

Dear Husband,

You are my best friend. Thank you for patiently loving us and for taking good care of our hearts and minds. Thank you for being gentle with us and understanding of our faults and loving us like Yeshua (Y'shua) does. You are a good man. I ♡ U

♡ **Love, Me**

Dear Husband,

Thank you for always listening to me. Thank you for understanding my love for you in the Almighty Lord God. Thank you for taking such good care of us. The world would be a better place if everyone created and generated peace and trust like you do. Shalom. P.S. I love your face.

♡ **Love, Me**

To the Breath and Life Eternal that cometh from the Lord of all,

Thank you for my husband and his gentle, strong, loving hand over our lives. Thank you that he loves us and that he looks to you in the "I AM" for his strength, power, peace and answers. I know deep in my soul that you are pleased with him. I appreciate that you bless him as you do. We know and appreciate that "I AM"; the Lord God of all guides us.

♡ **Love, Me**

Dear husband,

Thank you for taking wonderful care of us. You are an amazing husband who always puts our family first. I'm thankful that we are under the cover of the "I AM" while we stand in your authority.

I'm thankful for your love and attention. It is so good. ♡ You are the best husband.

♡ **Love, Me**

Hello.

You are my kind loving husband. Your authority is appreciated, and your wisdom is desired. We adore you. Thank you for loving us. ♡ Our anniversary is tomorrow! Yay, I'm excited to love you forever.

♡ **Love, Me**

Dear Husband,

I love your respectful and generous spirit.

$\heartsuit$ **Love, Me**

Father Lord God of All,

Thank you for my beautiful husband. You have made him in every perfect way. He is my king and lord, under your grace, and in the most perfect way. We praise you, Father. We honor you and all that you've done to show us your love and mercy.

Shalom

$\heartsuit$ **Love, Me**

Dear sweet husband,

I'm secretly admiring your wisdom and patience with me. I love how you speak. You are so wise, and you know the most loving and supportive things to say, anytime. I love looking into your eyes.

And I love being with you. You're my best friend. Thank you for loving us so well under grace and in the most perfect way of the Father, Lord God of all. Shalom.

$\heartsuit$ **Love, Me**

My love,

You are my favorite person. I love your company in your face and your voice. Your authority is my home. You are the very best husband and I appreciate all the things you do for me and our family. Our Heavenly Father: Lord God of all, is in you as "I AM" and I love to see you aligning yourself to be one with the Father. You are my hero. You are so brilliant. I ♡ U

♡ **Love, Me**

Dear Husband,

You are so funny. I love everything you say and do, and I raise up a shout of praise for your happiness. May you find the Lord's humor all day, every day, in joy for the rest of your life and eternity. **I know** God is so pleased with you. Shalom.

♡ **Love, Me**

Father God,

Thank you for my wonderful, kind husband. Thank you for his diligence and intelligence, emotionally and mentally. He takes such good care of us and teaches us with love. It is so easy to see you, Lord Father, in my husband's eyes and actions. Thank you for giving me the sight to see your nature in others.

My husband is a brilliant hero.

♡ **Love, Me**

Dear Husband,

I am so thankful that you are wise and that you are always interested in learning new things.

♡ **Love, Me**

Father Lord God of all,

Thank you for being kind and for always being gracious to us. Your love is so beautiful, and I am so thankful to be David's wife as we follow you. Thank you. I ♡ U.

Shalom

♡ **Love, Me**

Dear sweet husband,

Thank you for always caring about my feelings and for always finding ways to be nice to me. Thank you for learning and growing with me. You are the best husband in the world. I adore you.

♡ **Love, Me**

Dear Husband,

You are intelligent and gentle. Your voice comforts and encourages me to be the best person that I can be. Thank you for speaking to me gently and for disciplining me in love.

Love, Me

Dear Husband,

You are the most wonderful man that I have ever known. You live in a way that I really appreciate and respect. It is easy to honor you even when I make mistakes, because I **want** to honor you. Because of **who** you are. You are with the "I AM", and I see it more and more every day. To the source of all eternal creation is visibly within you all the time. You are so delicious.

I love you. You are my hero.

♡ **Love, Me**

Dear Husband,

Thank you for involving yourself in things that I am interested in. Thank you for letting me be included in the things that you care about. I love spending time with you and learning new things together.

♡ **Love, Me**

Dearest friend and adored husband,

I am so proud of you. You are the most wonderful example to us of a powerful and kind man. Thank you for teaching us about grace + mercy + for loving us so well.

I ♡ U

Love, Me

Dear Life of Mine,

I appreciate a husband who honors alignment and wisdom and grace in all that he does. I appreciate the time that I get to be with my husband, every day, as he leads our family. I appreciate our peaceful home. Shalom.

Love, Me

Dear Husband,

You make me feel loved and cherished in a way that no one else can. Your kind heart and gentle spirit make me fall in love with you more and more each day.

Love, Me

Write Love Notes

Visit www.feelslikefun.com/lovenotes/

Feels Like Fun® Publishing

www.ingramcontent.com/pod-product-compliance
Lightning Source LLC
Chambersburg PA
CBHW070028030426
42335CB00017B/2333